Compliments for Shirley Raye Redmond and Jennifer McKerley

"You just inspire people to get out and write (and submit)!"

—Robin, newspaper reporter

"That is just what is neat—you are not stingy with your knowledge!"

—Sally, librarian

"You presented so much practical information on the business side of writing…"

—Syble, history instructor

"Shirley Raye has the gift of mesmerizing her audiences with her practical advice, specific tips for getting published, and her quick wit and humor. She inspires, encourages, and provides the tools for success. Writers who follow her techniques GET published and have a great time along the way!"

—Bev, school teacher

"Jennifer motivates people to persevere. When she told the process of how she sold her first book, I realized I could do it too. I especially appreciated the detailed help on research, writing with a child's perspective in mind, and how to produce a manuscript with kid appeal."

—Richard, systems analyst

D1601827

Write a
Marketable
Children's Book
in 7 Weeks

Write a Marketable Children's Book in 7 Weeks

Shirley Raye Redmond and Jennifer McKerley

Langdon Street Press

212 3RD Avenue North, Suite 290

Minneapolis, MN 55401

612.455.2293

www.langdonstreetpress.com

ISBN - 978-1-934938-95-9

ISBN - 1-934938-95-5

LCCN - 2010928594

Cover Design by Alan Pranke

Typeset by James Arneson

Printed in the United States of America

Contents

Getting
Started

Now is the Time for You to Write a Children's Book

Were you one of those kids that loved to curl up with a good book? If so, you may have dreamed of writing a children's book of your own. It's a dream many people have. Yet very few do it.

<u>Now is the time for you to take action and fulfill your dream</u>.

Free up about two hours a day for seven weeks, and you can finish a marketable book for kids. We've used this method 30 times to write manuscripts that sold to major publishers, such as Random House, Simon & Schuster, and Gale Cengage. Some of our titles have even won contests and awards. You can use our plan to write a picture book, a chapter book, a reader, a middle grade nonfiction book, or a middle grade novel in seven weeks.

You Can Craft a Marketable Book in Less Than Two Months

We'll provide the "how to."

You provide the determination and elbow grease.

But the key to success is YOU.

No more procrastination. No more excuses.

Today is the day. Start here. Right now.

> You don't find the time to write a book.
> You MAKE the time.

Published writers have no more hours in their day to write than you do. Even the mega-authors on the *New York Times* Best-Seller list have deaths in the family, leaky roofs, rebellious teenagers, illness, and car trouble to contend with. They work around these inconveniences. You can too.

Free your schedule and start now!

Your First Assignment

Pledge to eliminate time-wasters. Go TV-free four nights a week.

Schedule 15 hours per week in an appointment book for your project.

Week 1:   Learn about the market. Read sample books.

Week 2:   Plot and plan.

Weeks 3-5: Write at least 5 pages every day.

Week 6:   Do more marketing research.

Week 7:   Revise.

The longest type of book you should write for this project is a middle grade novel—average length 25,000 words. You can complete it by writing five double-spaced manuscript pages each day for three weeks. You can certainly finish a shorter manuscript such as a picture book, a reader, a chapter book, or a nonfiction middle grade book in that same amount of time.

The Truth About Breaking In

We'll cover fiction writing in this workbook, but you need to know your best chance of getting published is with nonfiction. Why? Because fiction cycles through soft markets. The picture book market is often glutted, and editors don't want to see novels that are *Harry Potter* knock-offs.

Jennifer broke in with nonfiction. Years ago at a conference, she heard an editor say Random House wanted manuscripts for their Step into Reading line. The editor also said, "We always need true stories for kids." Later Jennifer learned from the editor that they were open to dog and horse stories at that time. Jennifer visited the library and read dozens of nonfiction readers published by Random House and other publishers. She learned the format, sentence structure, word usage, and subjects covered and how readers differed from publishing house to publishing house, but she focused on Random House's Step into Reading line.

She chose the famous horse Man o' War to write about because she found only one reader about a racehorse (which was about Seabiscuit). It was by a publisher other than Random House. Jennifer wrote her story for a higher level than the book which was currently on the market. When she submitted to Random House, she stated in her cover letter what the competition was and that her story featured a different horse and targeted older readers.

> You must write a strong story that stands on
> its own and fills a market need.

Multiply Profits With Nonfiction

Joyce Milton's reader *Dinosaur Days* has sold more than one million copies and gone into more than 50 printings since it was first published in 1985. Shirley Raye's first nonfiction titles, *Lewis & Clark: a Prairie Dog for the President* and *Tentacles! Tales of the Giant Squid* (both published by Random House), have sold over 150,000 copies each. Jennifer had similar success with *Amazing Armadillos* which was published by Random House in 2009. Less than three months after the book's release, Random House licensed the title to Scholastic Book Clubs, Inc., which made an initial purchase of 51,816 copies for their book club and school fairs. Few picture books or middle grade novels have such success. According to bookstore owners, if a fictional children's book doesn't "make it big" within nine months of release, it won't ever.

An editor at Random House once lamented that many writers don't write nonfiction for children because "it isn't glamorous." Perhaps it isn't. But we've found it to be as challenging and enjoyable as fiction, as well as being profitable.

Motivated to Write Fiction?

> If your dreams and ideas lead you to write fiction, then do it.
>
> Some fiction books become great successes.
>
> <u>They might as well be yours!</u>

Shirley Raye's first published children's book was a middle grade novel. She got the idea while speaking to grade school students about writing careers. Youngsters were intrigued by the term "ghost writer," and her no-nonsense explanation of the word always seemed to disappoint them. She was intrigued by their fascination with the word, then she wondered—what would happen if a couple of kids, knowing full well what a professional ghost writer is, advertised for one in the newspaper, but got a ghost of the Halloween variety instead? Would they be scared? Skeptical or delighted? How would they relate to the ghost?

These questions led her to write *Grampa and the Ghost* (which was published by Avon's Camelot Books). The title even became a *Weekly Reader* selection, but it disappeared from stores in less than a year. The royalties she earned all went back to the publisher to reimburse them for her advance. Still, the novel helped her get a foot in the door of the publishing world.

Discover the Magic of Kid Appeal

Whether fiction or nonfiction, a manuscript must have kid appeal. Before your manuscript can be transformed into a bound book sitting on a bookstore shelf, it must run a gauntlet. First, it must interest an editor. Then the editor will try to convince an editorial board and marketing execs that your book will make money.

Not sure if your idea has what it takes? Search online for popular titles for children, or visit bookstores to see what's selling. Werewolves have had streaks of popularity, and children often like skateboarding themes. But there are no new adventures of *Betsy-Tacy and Tibb* or *The Five Little Peppers*.

You may have a great manuscript,

but if it doesn't appeal to today's kids, an editor will not buy it.

You can appeal to kids today with a story that:

- Has a sense of fun and joy.

- Carries children into the magic of the moment.

- Makes kids feel at home in the tale.

- Portrays situations kids relate to:

    Succeeding after failing

    Belonging versus not fitting in

    Doing right versus doing wrong to gain approval

    Independence versus dependence

    Security versus insecurity

    Delayed rewards versus instant gratification

    Winning and losing

    Loss, separation, and reunion

    Rivalry and jealousy

You can capture your readers with a picture book that:

- Has great heart.
- Draws kids and adults.
- Tempts readers to turn the page.
- Has rhythm or a refrain.
- Has characters that are fully formed and likable.
- Has a logical progression of events.
- Has natural, unforced dialogue.
- Has vibrant descriptions.
- Has creative and original elements or a new twist.

Your Opportunities Abound

Think back to the subjects that fascinated you as a child—was it trains, adventures, monsters, fossils? They draw kids today too. Yet many new writers dismiss a marketable topic because they think all the "good ones have been taken." But creative thinking separates the published from the unpublished.

The solution?

> Discover a new angle to an old idea.
> Target a common topic to a different age group.

When Shirley Raye wrote her reader, *Lewis & Clark: A Prairie Dog for the President*, there were already many children's books on the subject of Lewis and and Clark. However, there were none in the reader lines for grades 1-3. Nor was there a book that focused on the explorers' adventures in capturing and delivering a live prairie dog to President Thomas Jefferson. Her manuscript put a new twist on a story from history, and it filled a market niche.

The Scoop About Illustrations

> Most publishers do not want a manuscript submitted with illustrations unless the author also does the drawings.

Do not find someone to illustrate your manuscript and make an agreement. Most publishers hire an illustrator after a manuscript has been purchased.

However, for historical fiction and nonfiction books, it is helpful for writers to keep a list of sources that have photos or pictures that can help an illustrator. The list would not be submitted with the manuscript. If the story were to sell, the writer would let the editor know that useful sources are available to pass along to the illustrator. For Jennifer's *Man o' War* reader, she provided website links and picture sources to the editor which showed Man o' War's racing colors, an old video of the horse running, and photos of his owner and trainer.

The Skinny On Rhyme

> Rhyming readers and picture books are hard to sell.

Some guidelines for publishers and literary agencies in *Writer's Market* and *Markets for Children's Writers* specify they do not want rhyming texts. This is because editors and agents receive many poorly done submissions in rhyme. Shirley Raye and Jennifer have more than 30 books on the market, but each of them has sold only one rhyming text (*The Princesses' Lucky Day* and *There Goes Turtle's Hat*, which were released by Picture Window Books).

Prose can be lyrical, and you can create rhythm without rhyme. You can certainly use prose to instill the magical ingredients of heart and kid appeal. You can use repetition, alliteration, and patterns—like the common pattern of three events or major actions. When you complete this workbook, if you still feel your story is best told in rhyme, get an English textbook and study scansion.

Jennifer was told by an agent that "ABC" texts are also hard to sell. We will not teach about writing rhyme or ABC books.

Seize the Market

This course is designed to help you write a sellable children's book. There are other books that teach how to write and how to write fast. The key word for our lessons is MARKETABLE.

However, keep your readers' age level in mind as you chose your topic. The life of serial killer Ted Bundy may be a marketable subject for adults, but it is not a marketable topic for children. Even if it were, it is not suitable. Be market savvy and also be morally responsible to young readers.

We've based this course on techniques that work for us, and we've sold more than 30 books. We cannot guarantee your book will sell, but ours did.

We can guarantee you'll learn what goes into creating a marketable children's book. And at the end of seven weeks, you'll have a completed manuscript. We hope your journey launches you into the writing habit and the writing life.

Get Ready. Buckle Up. Go!

Assignment

Read this whole book through. It will take you about
one hour and will give you an idea of what's ahead.

Week 1

Unravel the Mysteries of the Market

This week you will research children's books and the market. This step is every bit as important as the actual weeks of writing and revision.

Shirley Raye always scopes out the market before a new project. Years ago she got an idea for a nonfiction book by reading Richard Ellis's *The Search for the Giant Squid: The Biology and Mythology of the World's Most Elusive Sea Creature*. Recalling her own childhood interests, she knew inquisitive youngsters would relish a book about this fascinating creature. She spent her planning week in bookstores and the children's section of the local library. Her research revealed there was no nonfiction reader for grades 2-4 about the squid.

She read dozens of books aimed at kids in this age category. She studied the diction and sentence structure. She counted words, paragraphs, and pages. This intensive market analysis provided her with a suitable blueprint or pattern—a 48-page book of 950 words. She also compiled a list of publishers that had already released books similar in style to the one she intended to write. Then she wrote *Tentacles! Tales of the Giant Squid* and sold it to Random House!

> Like Shirley Raye, you need a plan.

If you were going to take a trip across the country, you would plan your route, how long you'd be on the road, what sights to see, where you wanted to spend more time, when the trip would end, etc. Although you know trips often have unexpected stops and detours, you would still start with a plan. So don't skip market research or the planning weeks, and <u>don't skimp on note taking</u>.

> The success of the 7-week plan lies in organization and careful planning.
> It works for us!

It's time to research the market and identify your target group.

Goals of market research:

1: To decide what book category you should aim for.

2: To learn about the market and publishers.

3: To create a guide or template for your book.

Assignment

If you know what category you want to aim for,
do an online search of children's books for your subject—
for instance: "bigfoot legends myths children's books."

---

bigfoot legends myths children's books   Search

Advanced Search
Preferences

If you are writing fiction, you can't do a precise search, but any info will be helpful—"mystery, buried treasure, first pet, tooth fairy, fun on the farm," etc. Also search booksellers' websites. If your idea is a "first trip on an airplane" picture book, are there four out there already? If so, you should come up with a new angle, unless you have expertise that gives your manuscript extra clout.

Don't worry if there's some competition. You <u>will</u> find similar books. If you're lucky, when you find them in the online databases, you will see "Out of Print" by the titles. If they had good sales, editors might buy another book on the topic. If similar books are still in print, it's up to you to point out to the editors how your manuscript differs and why your publisher should buy another novel about a boy wizard.

Assignment

Go to the library with this book and paper and pen. Explore the categories and decide what category and age group you should aim for.

Age range and word count vary depending on the publisher.

Categories:

<u>Picture book fiction</u>: Ages 4 to 8; 100 to 1,000 words. Picture books are designed to be read <u>to</u> children. Illustrations supply information that is omitted in the text, such as the color of someone's hair (unless color is important to state).

Picture book nonfiction: Ages 4 to 8; 100 to 1,000 words. Many nonfiction picture books are illustrated with photographs or stock art.

Storybook, fiction and nonfiction: Ages 8 to 12; 900 to 2,000 words. Storybooks are picture books for older kids. Although they are illustrated, the text stands alone and doesn't require pictures to complete the story.

Concept picture book: Up to age 8; 100 to 1,000 words. These books teach concepts such as compare/contrast and sequence (days of the week and ABCs).

Picture book bio: Ages 8 to 12; 1,000 to 2,000 words. These are biographies of famous people that kids will read about in school because the people are tied to school curricula and current events.

Reader or Easy to Read, fiction and nonfiction: Grades pre-K to 4; 400 to 2,000 words. The purpose of readers is to instill a love of reading, and they are written so children can read the books themselves.

Chapter book, fiction and nonfiction: Ages 7 to 10; 2,500 to 5,000 words. Unlike picture books for younger readers, a chapter book tells the story primarily through prose, rather than pictures. Still, chapter books often have illustrations. This category represents the level at which children first read books that are divided into chapters.

Middle grade nonfiction: Ages 9 to 12; 2,000 to 10,000 words. These titles cover science, history, biographies, cultural topics, etc. They are often illustrated with stock photos, maps, and graphs.

<u>Middle grade novel</u>: Ages 9 to 12; 15,000 to 50,000 words. These texts have few if any illustrations. The text supplies all the information.

Assignment

Now that you know your category and age group, use the following checklist to acquaint yourself thoroughly with similar books.

<u>Checklist</u>

_____ Search the library's catalog for books in your category and age range that are similar to your subject. Scan through those books and keep some to check out. For example, if you are writing about an invention or an inventor, look at bios and stories about inventions.

_____ Use out-of-print books to find ideas that could be refreshed. Use books still in print to know what is on the market. Use <u>all</u> the books to discover an angle that hasn't been covered for your age level. There may be something briefly mentioned in a book that you could elaborate on. Remember how Shirley Raye focused on the prairie dog to give her Lewis and Clark reader a unique slant? Look for ways to offer a new twist on an old idea.

_____ Ask the librarian what the most checked-out and requested books are in your category. Read them to discover why they are popular.

<u>Use the following forms to analyze 5 books similar to what you want to write.</u>

Your idea _____

Fiction or nonfiction _____

Age Range _____

Book category _____

Are there titles similar to your book?

Library   Yes _____   No _____

Local bookstores   Yes _____   No _____

Online search   Yes _____   No _____

List books and publishers:

Title   Publisher

1._____   _____

2. _____   _____

3. _____   _____

4. _____   _____

5. _____   _____

Estimates	Book 1	Book 2	Book 3	Book 4	Book 5
Number of major characters	____	____	____	____	____
Word count	____	____	____	____	____
Number of chapters, if any	____	____	____	____	____
Pages per book	____	____	____	____	____
Average pages per chapter	____	____	____	____	____
Lines of dialogue in sample chapter	____	____			
Lines of description in sample chap.	____	____			
Action paragraphs in sample chapter	____	____			
Anecdotes in sample chapter (nonfiction)	____	____			

Assignment

Using *Writer's Market* or *Book Markets for Children's Writers*,
look up the publishers of the five books you analyzed.
Note submission guidelines, editors' names, and website addresses.
(These reference books are available in most libraries.)

The Key to Plotting

This week you will plan and plot. Many writers get bogged down in the middle of their book or lost near the end, and we want you to avoid this problem. Perhaps you've had a manuscript rejected by an editor who wrote, "This story lacks clarity." What does that mean, you wonder? It means that you didn't really know what you were writing about, so the editor didn't either.

Take the time to map your course. You're on a journey. When you feel you're getting lost, you can pull out your "plot map."

Even if you're planning to write a nonfiction book, we recommend you read this section on plotting. Many of our suggestions on character development, action, and conflict will help you build your nonfiction story arc or narrative thread, which we discuss later on pages 34-36.

For fiction and nonfiction, you need a plot map. So what is a plot map?

A plot map has five necessary plot points that make up a story.

CHARACTER + ACTION + CONFLICT + CLIMAX + RESOLUTION

Although setting, animated dialogue, emotional tension, and suspense add to a story's interest, you don't have a story until you have the five plot basics. Some writers start by deciding on a theme (what a book is about). Then they identify a premise (what they want to say about the theme). We feel a plot map is more practical and to the point.

Assignment

Write the five plot points at the top of a large index card.
CHARACTER + ACTION + CONFLICT + CLIMAX + RESOLUTION

Create Characters Readers Care About

"I have someone I want you to meet." Have you ever had someone say that to you—a friend or family member perhaps? Could you tell that she was eager for you to like her friend, favorite teacher, or boyfriend as much as she did? This is the same eagerness you must bring to introducing a character to readers.

Your character must have depth. Some people use the image of onion layers or a multilayered dessert to illustrate the layers of a character's personality. You cannot write about a run-of-the-mill character. Take the time to construct a memorable one. When youngsters talk about books, they refer to them by the characters' names. They like Nancy Drew and Harry Potter. They want a pet pig like Wilbur or a rabbit like Bunnicula. When we get fan mail from young readers, they never mention dialogue or conflict resolution. They write about a character.

"I think G.I. Joe was the bravest pigeon of all."

"I love Man o' War because he goofed up, but he kept trying."

"Dicey Langston is my favorite heroine of 1776."

Assignment

Make a personality card for each character. Fill out a
5 x 8 index card for each person in your book, listing
everything about them from birthdays to birthmarks.

Shirley Raye cuts photos of people from catalogs and magazines. While writing, she can refer to the photo to remind herself if the character has blue eyes or short brown hair or braids.

Shirley Raye endows many of her characters with quirks. Tallulah, the lovable ghost in *Grampa and the Ghost*, calls everybody by some other name, usually a silly one. Yet when it comes to spelling accurately, she's a regular floating *Webster's Dictionary*. Such idiosyncrasies give fictional characters a touch of real humanity. This is particularly important when writing fantasy or science fiction. Even though your characters may be talking beavers, like the ones in C.S. Lewis's *The Lion, the Witch and the Wardrobe*, they must act human if young readers are going to care about them.

Know everything about your protagonist or main character. Why do you like this character? Do you understand his motivation for doing what he does?

> If a character is going to persist to achieve a goal in the end,
>
> we must know what's driving him.

A character must have moral fiber and a backbone, even if he's shy or bad in math. After all, you want young readers to admire the protagonist. If not, why would they connect with him and stick with him when conflict occurs?

People of all ages love, fear, dread, and hate. There are things they desire—things they are curious about. People also do mundane everyday things. Use the mundane only when it advances the plot or fleshes out your character. Use unusual or dramatic aspects to mark a turn in someone's life, while you advance the plot. New experiences can reveal things a character hadn't realized about herself and still be consistent with the character the reader knows. Use such turning points to emphasize your character's strengths or weaknesses.

Questions to help put flesh on the bones of main characters:

- Who or what does the character love?

- What does the character fear the most?

- What worries the character?

- What does the character wish would happen?

- What does he or she daydream about?

- How does the character move, sit, or run?

- What does he or she do when nervous, excited, or scared?

- What are three things the character likes to do?

- What are two personality traits?

- What are two strengths and two weaknesses?

- How is the character going to change or grow after dealing with the conflict in the story? (Is he going to feel more confident? Is she going to learn something about family or friends?)

Questions to help round out secondary characters:

- What does the character wish would happen—or not happen?

- What is something the character likes to do?

- What are two personality traits?

- What is one strength? One weakness?

Think Action!

You know what an "action film" is, right? Well, you need to have an "action story." Characters must do more than think and talk and plan. Your book will compete with videos, computer games, soccer practice, CDs, skateboarding, and youth activities. An editor knows that. So she's looking for something that will tempt a child to read. Even a beginning reader like *The Cat in the Hat* by Dr. Seuss has lots of action. One dreadful thing after another happens, resulting in a shocking mess near the end. Think of "action" in terms of bodily movements, not conflict. Still, action does not have to be exploits in the "kung-fu" sort of way.

> Action is first prompted by a goal, then it's prompted by conflict that blocks that goal; even minor conflict—like a thirsty toddler being told he's not big enough to get a drink on his own.

Captivate with Conflict

How do you keep readers glued to the page? Test your character with rising disasters or setbacks. Make your character struggle. Make readers worry.

> Conflict is opposition. It is a series of brick walls your character hits while attempting to reach a big goal.

Conflict is the necessary core of the story. It is what gives a story meaning. Give your main characters something vital to attempt, conquer, battle, solve, or survive. Build the story (and action) around one clear external conflict your main character must overcome.

There are external conflicts: characters against nature, against circumstances, and against other characters. There are internal conflicts: a character against himself, as he tries to gain confidence to reach a dream, deals with smoldering resentment, or faces an unexpressed fear. If you have both kinds of conflict, weave the internal struggle throughout the story as the character fights the external conflict.

Make the conflict important. It cannot be "token" conflict for the sake of tension. It must be of real significance.

> Conflict must threaten the achievement of the character's goal.

Naturally, the older your target audience, the more intense the conflict can be. You don't want to write a picture book for 4-year-olds that places the main character in a life-or-death situation. However, it may be a great plot premise for 14-year-old readers.

Before you decide what the conflict in the story will be, you'll need to ask more questions about your main character.

Assignment

Answer these questions on the card for your main character:
- WHO is my main character?
- WHAT does she want?
- WHY does she want it?
- WHERE will she find it?
- WHEN will she get it?
- HOW will she get it?

There are also some conflict no-nos to avoid when plotting your story.

> Mom and Dad, Grandpa, favorite teachers, and coaches should not solve the character's problems. Your character must do it herself or himself.

If you have a hard time keeping busybodies out of your story outline, get rid of them until you've successfully plotted your course and then add them back in as supporting characters.

There's an old maxim about "conflict building character." It applies to fiction too. Your main character should grow emotionally, physically, mentally, or spiritually after dealing with the conflict in the story. That's why you can't allow any interference on the part of those well-meaning adults. Another no-no: the threat in the story cannot be caused by chance, bad luck, or fate. However, natural disasters can cause conflict and danger.

At Last, It's Here—the Climax

The climax is the emotional center of the story.

> You've reached the story climax when your character feels a sense of hopelessness and wonders if she'll ever reach her all-important goal.

It's at this point that she musters her last ounce of courage, strength, and determination to try once again—despite great odds. As you near the climax, make the scenes brief and use short sentences with active verbs to increase the story's pace.

Resolve and Satisfy

You must successfully resolve everything in the final scene. Don't leave loose ends dangling. You don't want to quit your story abruptly, which is often a problem for beginning writers who get distracted, tired, or bored with their project and are too eager to send it off to an editor. When you're finished, you should read your story all the way through in one sitting. Make sure you've answered: who, what, when, where, why, and how? In other words, you don't want an editor to get to the end of your book and ask, "But who…? Or "And when…? Or "Then why…?"

> Successful conflict resolution is essential in children's books.

Don't confuse "successful" or "satisfying" with "happy." Not all books have happy endings. Consider *Charlotte's Web*. The spider heroine dies in the end, but young readers are comforted by the knowledge that her spider daughters will live in the barn and watch over Wilbur.

Assignment

Now draft the five story points on your plot map.

The following is a sample plot map for portions of the main storyline in the well-known tale *The Wonderful Wizard of Oz* by Lyman Frank Baum. Notice that each conflict prompts a new action.

CHARACTER	ACTION	CONFLICT	CLIMAX	RESOLUTION
Dorothy wants to go home Needs help →	Travels to Oz →	Witch sends obstacles ←		
	D wins Wiz sends her to kill Witch →	D captured by Witch ←		
	D melts Witch →	D still can't get home ←		
	Tries to fly on monkey→	Defeats foes But no way home →	Shoes are the way home →	D reunited with family

---

Assignment

If you have a subplot, draft in the plot points for it, as well.

There are two plotting aids on the next few pages that can be used along with your plot map. The first is an outline that Jennifer used to write the 32-page reader *Rules of the Net* (released in 2009 by Picture Window Books) for grades K-2. The second is a plot grid she made for her middle grade novel-in-progress *House of Snakes.*

Plot outline used for a 32-page story for grades K-2:

Pages 4-5:	Setup. 3 characters. Some action. All is well.
Pages 6-7:	Characters in typical situation. Action. All is well.
Pages 8-9:	New situation. Action reveals something about relationships.
Pages 10-11:	Problem develops with main character and 1st secondary character. Minor consequences. Reveal more about relationships.
Pages 12-13:	Problem develops with main character and 2nd secondary character. Minor, growing consequences. Reveal more about relationships.
Pages 14-15:	Greater consequences for main and 1st secondary.
Pages 16-17:	Greater consequences for main and 2nd secondary.
Pages 18-19:	Discussion of problem by main and at least one other character.
Pages 20-21:	Decide on possible solution.
Pages 22-23:	Act on solution. Doesn't work.
Pages 24-25:	No solution seems possible to main character.
Pages 26-27:	Main character and maybe one other character try new idea.
Pages 28-29:	Goof up, but then…
Pages 30-31:	It works in the end. Solution.
Page 32:	Return to better-than-normal situation.

Plot Grid for *House of Snakes* by Jennifer McKerley

Chapters 1 – 4

1	2	3	4
Start mid scene. Major change/ event propels Main Character (MC) into new adventure, out-of-norm challenge, danger, or situation. Reveal some of personality. Describe MC briefly.	Establish Opposition (O). Introduce Main Supporting Character (MSC). Describe briefly. MC & MSC join forces and plot/ plan to overcome. Show personalities of MC and MSC.	MC & MSC act. New info arises. Include some background info about MC & other supporting characters (SC). New development occurs, and situation worsens.	Establish/develop MSC more. Begin subplot. Characters discuss big problem, which reveals much higher stakes, also reveals more about MC. MC (or with others) feels that maybe they cannot win.

Chapters 5 – 8

5	6	7	8
MC & MSC rally. Act to solve new development. They succeed and are empowered. MC & MSC decide on new course of action (false lead). Characters know they must race against time to make new action succeed.	MC & MSC pursue false lead. O intensifies. They act as clock ticks. Reveal important personality or character traits. Continue subplot begun in Chap. 4.	MC & MSC race against time. As they continue toward goal, MC pushed into confrontation with O. First intense scene of book which results in new disaster.	Continue scene from Ch. 7. O triumphs. MC discovers lead was false, and barely escapes from danger. MC & MSC reassure each other.

Chapters 9 – 12

9	10	11	12
O becomes stronger. Stakes raised. MC realizes O becomes much greater threat. Complicate and continue subplot.	MC loses determination, but gathers new info. MC & MSC decide goal is not worth it and almost give up. Again MC rallies. Main story goal renewed. MC/ MSC gain new grit. Move toward final game plan.	Subplot is resolved. MC and/or MSC act on final game plan. O also makes big move, and MSC thrown into danger/ distress.	MC intensifies efforts toward goal, but clock is ticking. MC must help MSC. MC confronts O, and puts self in danger to rescue MSC. Situation intensifies. MC tries to rescue MSC. Success not clear when chapter ends.

Chapters 13 – 16

13	14	15	16
MSC helped out of dilemma. Relief and joy brief because gaining freedom of MSC put MC in worse danger. MC and O on fast track to final showdown.	Action moves quickly toward final confrontation between MC & O. (Make scenes in rest of book short and use short sentences with active verbs to increase pace.) O makes ultimate move, which results in the biggest disaster yet for MC.	O seemingly has won. Offers MC a way out or part of spoils of victory if MC will do something bad. MC chooses right. Climax—greatest emotional struggle over right/wrong in story, or great escape from danger. O loses. MC wins.	MC & MSC make clear how victory made their lives better. Tie up any threads of subplot left. MC & MSC reap rewards. End mid-scene to make MC's story seem to go on.

Discover How to Write Fascinating Nonfiction

With nonfiction, your *who, what, when, where, how*, and *why* will be answered as you retell a true story in your own words. Yet you must structure your retelling to produce brisk pace and compelling drama. To do this, plan your story using the plot map with its five plot points. This will give your story an arc.

Assignment

Write the five plot points on an index card.

CHARACTER + ACTION + CONFLICT + CLIMAX + RESOLUTION

As you research your topic, look for the above elements in the true tale.

How to Craft Your Story Arc

A story arc is to nonfiction what plot is to fiction. Once you have chosen what person, animal, event, or thing you're going to write about, select specific events that build to a dramatic highlight or pivotal point in the true story.

In Jennifer's nonfiction reader, *Man o' War, Best Racehorse Ever*, her "character" (or subject) is Man o' War. She shows "action" and "conflict" by revealing how a wobbly colt becomes a successful racehorse. The story builds on Man o' War's early wins and on a seeming disaster—the race Man o' War started backwards. He redeems himself with win after win up to the climax, when Man o' War goes against the Triple Crown Winner—and wins. The resolution of the story arc is the horse's subsequent fame and retirement. The plot map for this nonfiction story follows.

CHARACTER	ACTION	CONFLICT	CLIMAX	RESOLUTION
Man o' War is wobbly colt →	Trainer tries →	MW fidgets ←		
	Old horse calms him MW wins races →	Starts race facing backwards- loses ←		
	Beats top horses Best race- horse in world →	No races Owners refuse-their horses will only lose ←		
	Races new horse and wins →	Then races Trip. Crown Winner →	Fans fret But MW wins →	Retires-fans still visit Named Greatest Horse of Cent.

Sometimes nonfiction is written using a narrative thread instead of a story arc. The technique is often used for books about animals. The author strings together what an animal typically does in a day or season or what a famous animal did in its lifetime, but does so in a way that gives the feel of a storyline. An author might relate the animal's journey from morning to night, from season to season, from place to place, or from birth to adulthood. Remember to write action scenes to show these activities.

Jennifer wrote *Amazing Armadillos* with a narrative thread. Instead of just listing the characteristics and habits of the animal, she arranged and paced typical events, such as escaping from danger, to create tension and dramatic peaks. She chronicled an armadillo's life through a year.

With nonfiction, there is a temptation to try to tell everything about a subject. You cannot. And an editor will not want to buy a book that merely repeats facts and information like an encyclopedia article. So you must select the most important <u>and the most fun</u> facts.

Remarkable and Real

You must bring real characters to life on paper.

In Shirley Raye's nonfiction reader, *The Dog that Dug for Dinosaurs* (which was published by Simon and Schuster), the main characters are Mary Anning and her dog Tray. The fact that Miss Anning became a famous British fossil collector in the early 1800s is true. She discovered the first *Ichthyosaurus* in 1821 and the first *Plesiosaurus* in 1823.

Yet Mary had to become more than just a person in history—she had to have personality, as well. In the middle of the book, a teenage Mary is watching tourists come to her home town of Lyme Regis to scramble along the shore and cliffs looking for dinosaur fossils. The men are wearing top hats and the women wear frilly bonnets and carry parasols. So that youngsters could identify with this teen who lived two centuries before, Shirley Raye used creative license to imagine something Mary logically could have said. It brought Mary's sense of humor to life on paper.

Mary shook her head and smiled. She rubbed Tray's soft ears. They watched the strangers together. "They don't have the right tools," Mary Ann whispered. "They are wearing the wrong kinds of shoes. Aren't they silly, Tray?" Tray yipped and chased his tail.

Make sure what you create is something that would have been likely and logical. Also, make sure it fits the style of sample books from the publishers you want to submit to. Some publishers do not allow creative license and want a writer to include only what can be documented. But, of course, such publishers still want writers to bring history to life with vivid portraits of people and events. Young readers enjoy amusing anecdotes that reveal the personalities of famous folks and the qualities that made them remarkable.

The Truth About What Kids Like

> Kids love the weird and the unusual.

When researching *The Alamo* (which Simon & Schuster released in 2004), Shirley Raye dug up interesting facts about children who died in the battle: The two young Wolf brothers were only eleven and twelve years old. Although their father pleaded with Mexican soldiers to spare their lives, the boys were heartlessly killed.

She also learned that the corpse of an unidentified black woman was found lying between two cannons near the wall. No one knows who she was or what she was doing inside the old mission. Shirley Raye included those historical tidbits in the book. When youngsters ask, "Did that really happen?" she nods her head and says, "Yes." The look of amazed satisfaction on their faces is a reward all its own.

Jennifer sold her *Amazing Armadillos* manuscript by emphasizing the creature's quirkiest traits: When startled, armadillos jump three to four feet straight up in the air; they can stand up and hop backwards; and they always bear quadruplets of the same sex.

Assignment

As you research, gather important facts,
but also collect quirky, interesting tidbits.

You may find a good beginning from the unusual, weird, scary, or amazing facts you record. Jennifer opened her nonfiction book *Goblins* (which Thomson Gale published in 2006) with a goblin legend from southern England in the 1830s. It told about a traveler in the night following someone ahead with a lantern. When the poor wayfarer goes over a cliff, he realizes he was following a goblin. The creature maliciously floats across the abyss while the man clings to the edge of the cliff. Starting a nonfiction book with a dramatic event, fun anecdote, or attention-getting fact grabs the reader.

Fashion a Fresh Approach

Some beginning writers hesitate to attempt nonfiction, thinking everything's been written about before. They mistakenly believe fiction is "more original."

Both of these assumptions are false—to a degree. No matter what fictional tale you might write, there are many other stories like it already. Consider the popularity of vampires, girl sleuths, and even pigs (Wilbur, Babe, Gordie, and Olivia, to name a few).

In nonfiction, if you're writing about a person or incident that has been written about many times before, consider a creative new approach to make your manuscript more marketable. Earlier we told how Shirley Raye found a different angle for the oft-told story of Lewis and Clark's expedition. She discovered this angle while on a trip to Yellowstone National Park. She picked up materials about the 1804 expedition and learned that the explorers had made a considerable effort to capture a living prairie dog to send back to Thomas Jefferson as a souvenir of their westward journey.

The image of the expedition's 40 grown men peering and reaching down into prairie dog burrows (while the prairie dogs watched curiously in the background) tickled her "inner child." It was that episode that she chose to focus on while writing her 48-page reader *Lewis and Clark: A Prairie Dog for the President*. She spent her research time discovering how the Corps of Discovery actually shipped the little creature back to Washington, D.C. This fresh approach on a true tale convinced Random House to buy her manuscript, and the book has sold well year after year.

The Answer to the Viewpoint Question

Write your story in First Person or Third Person Limited Omniscient. They are the most common viewpoints used for children's books.

First Person: A main character is the narrator, who speaks her thoughts to the reader (I heard … She told me …). The main character tells about her life, problems, dreams, etc. The story unfolds through her perspective. Author Kate DiCamillo uses the first person viewpoint in her middle grade novel, *Because of Winn Dixie.*

My name is India Opal Buloni, and last summer my daddy, the preacher, sent me to the store for a box of macaroni-and-cheese, some white rice and two tomatoes and I came back with a dog.

Third Person Limited Omniscient: The narrator takes the reader inside the main character's head, and the story unfolds through that character's eyes. The narrator refers to characters using third person pronouns such as he, she, it, and they. Third Person Limited Omniscient is the most common form in both fiction and nonfiction books for children. The reader does not get inside any other character's mind, and the narrator doesn't reveal any information the main character doesn't have access to. Jennifer used this viewpoint in *Rules of the Net.*

Kate glared at Carlos. He tried to talk to her, but she walked away. The next day as the game started, Kate sat on the bench. Carlos sat watching too. I hope Kate gets to play later, he thought.

The reader only knows what Carlos is thinking. The reader concludes that Kate is mad by her actions, but does not get inside Kate's mind.

Break Through—Even if You're Not an Expert

Although conventional wisdom says, "Write what you know," we knew nothing about giant squid, the jersey devil, or racehorses before we wrote on those topics. We researched and relied on the expertise of others.

> Do extensive research and take extensive notes—
> more than you think you'll need.

Keep records of all sources. Record a book's title, author's name, the page numbers you take notes from, the publishing house, the city where the house is located, publication date, and ISBN. Make a special note of where you find unusual information. If your book sells, the editor will pass on questions from copy editors to you. You want to back up any little-known fact with a reliable source. The Internet is a great blessing to writers, but use creditable websites sponsored by museums, educational institutions, or government agencies such as the Library of Congress. Most editors will not accept information from Wikipedia. Be sure to submit a bibliography with the manuscript.

Many publishers hire professionals in the field to "vet" or examine manuscripts for accuracy. Dr. Clyde Roper, a leading expert on giant squid, vetted Shirley Raye's manuscript about this mysterious sea creature. He even provided photos for the book. Lisa Bradley of the Museum of Texas Tech University vetted Jennifer's

Amazing Armadillos. This expert examination helps an editor and writer correct errors, and it gives the book academic clout.

Week 3

The Only Way to Fulfill Your Dream

The only way to be a writer is to write. Start now. Remember—in just five weeks, you'll have a completed manuscript.

Assignment

Write at least five pages every day.
Keep your character cards and plot map in sight. Don't worry about grammar, spelling, punctuation, or anything else. Simply write.

Go ahead and give in to the temptation to ramble on and on. Forget word limits and word choices. Want to write your ending first? Go ahead! If a particular scene comes to mind, and you're eager to put it on paper, do so. If you want, write the main storyline only, then go back and add a subplot. You can stitch everything together later. Refer to the "Estimates" sheet on page 20 to provide a guide for a minimum amount per chapter of dialogue, action scenes, etc., but don't let it limit you or slow you down. Every journey should include Rest Stops, and we have provided those along the way. So pull over now and then and take a break.

REST STOP

How to Deliver Great Dialogue

Simply put, dialogue is "conversations between characters." Dialogue serves two purposes: it moves the plot forward, and it reveals personality and character traits. Don't tell us that Becky argued with her mother. Show us in dialogue. If Danny is always grumpy and out-of-sorts, show us by the way he speaks to other characters. In fiction, you create dialogue that suits the age, personality, region, and educational level of the characters you have created.

Write dialogue that is:

- Age appropriate in vocabulary and level of thought.
- Natural sounding. (Listen to how real children talk.)
- Varied in sentence length.
- Different for different characters.
- Revealing about character and personality.
- Not overloaded with dialect or slang.
- Attached to taglines ("Blah," Jane said).

In writing for adults, tag lines are often left out, but it's important not to take the chance of confusing children.

> Only omit tag lines when it's perfectly clear who's speaking:
>
> "I'm bigger than you," Shelly told Jill.
>
> Jill shook her head. "You are not."
>
> "Am too."
>
> "Are not."
>
> "Am too!" Shelly screamed.

If one character says something startling ("I stole money from Dad's wallet."), make sure the other character reacts in dialogue. Many beginning writers simply go on with the story. Real life isn't like that. When someone admits something astonishing, you at least say, "What? You're kidding!"

Don't let one character get all the lines of dialogue.

> Chatty scenes should be like a good tennis match between equal players—back and forth, back and forth, brisk and interesting.

There's a goal in a tennis match. The players want to win the game. In a way, there's a goal in conversation too. Why are they talking? Are the characters exchanging information? Is one trying to comfort or encourage the other? But don't use rambling dialogue to fill up pages to make the word count right.

Dialogue doesn't take place in a vacuum either. Some writers show us the conversation—*he said, she said*, but we don't know WHERE the conversation is taking place. Is it in a gym, a secret cave in the forest, or at a baseball game?

Writing nonfiction? You can still use dialogue, relying on actual quotes from letters, diaries, and other sources. You cannot reveal everything about a historical figure, so choose wisely to present the most interesting account and heartfelt aspects. Nonfiction by necessity requires third person viewpoint and past tense, which puts more distance between the reader and the story. Choose quotes that help create drama and tension and reveal your character more fully.

REST STOP

Ban Author Intrusion

Does your 6-year-old protagonist use colloquialisms like, "Stars and garters, I'm tired!" or phrases such as, "For your information, I'm a member of Brownie Troop 222!"? Then you've got a problem. Dialogue needs to be realistic.

> Put yourself in the head of a youngster and write like one.

Ask yourself: "Is the word choice age-appropriate? Would a 7-year-old or 1st grader use such a word? Or is it the adult author talking?"

Author intrusion is as annoying and as obvious as a door-to-door salesman sticking his foot in the front door so you can't close it. Get out of there! Don't give your readers speeches, sermons, or a card catalog of references and research sources. People don't talk that way, and kids will get bored.

REST STOP

Grip Your Readers With Emotion

> Like mortar between bricks, emotion stabilizes your narrative.

Children are emotional creatures. Young readers want to be scared with your characters. When characters take a brave step, readers want to feel the exhilaration with them. They want to conquer everyday troubles with characters they care about.

So let your characters giggle, worry, and even weep. Mark and Sibyl experience a wide range of emotions in *Grampa and the Ghost*, including anxiety, fear, delight, and affection. If your story must have a sad ending, such as two friends parting, at least make it hopeful, so readers can imagine that the friends will meet again one day.

> Keep in mind that for every action in your story,
> there must be an emotional reaction.

Here's where your character cards will come in handy. If you're not sure how your characters will respond to something, reconsider the personality traits you've recorded for each character. One character may cry when disappointed, while another one may sulk. Don't use emotion to "beef up" a dull plot. In other words, the protagonist and her friend shouldn't have a shouting match at the end of Chapter 4, simply because you can't think of anything else for them to do. The emoting has to be real and honest.

Consider the real kids you know. Some cry when they are stressed. Others get grumpy. Some chew their nails and get very quiet. Still others eat everything in sight and talk too fast and too much.

> Your characters must have emotional responses
> that are believable to the reader.

An editor will probably not buy a book in which a 5-year-old behaves stoically following the accidental death of his beloved pet. A character's maturity level will influence the way he responds emotionally to conflict in the story. A 6-year-old and a 16-year-old will handle confrontation with a bully differently.

Week
4

The Most Dangerous Time of All

If you're prone to procrastinate, this will be your most dangerous week. Don't let your willpower wane. Take your craft and <u>yourself</u> seriously.

Will power is defined as the "ability to carry out one's decisions." Unfortunately, will power is not something you're born with. Writers must develop and hone this ability if they are to achieve their goals. Hang in there!

> Professionalism and perseverance are more often the keys
> to writing success than talent or originality.

Be your own merciless drill instructor. Concentrate only on each day's goal.

<u>Assignment</u>

Working on a longer manuscript?
Produce your five pages each day.

If you've been working on a shorter manuscript—48 pages or less—you may already be done with your second draft. What now?

Assignment

Improve and polish that draft into a better one.
This time you must separate the wheat from the chaff.

Don't edit or tackle grammar errors at this time. You'll do that during Week 7. Now you want to focus on quality control. Get rid of anecdotes or scenes that do not move your story forward. Concentrate on the "why" of it all. Why are you writing this story? To inform? Inspire? Entertain? Instruct? Does each page or chapter reflect your purpose? Does the dialogue enhance the plot or pace of your story? If not, get rid of it.

REST STOP   **Avoid Lapses in Logic**

Your young readers <u>will</u> notice any lapses in logic. Kids are young, not dumb. In Shirley Raye's chapter book *Grampa and the Ghost*, the Gaffney youngsters rebel against the very idea of ghosts, while their grandfather readily accepts Tallulah's spooky presence. Shirley Raye knew savvy young readers would wonder why. While Mark openly admits he doesn't believe in ghosts, and Sibyl is a bit scared and skeptical, Grampa Will takes it all in stride. Young readers would wonder about this. The matter had to be addressed. Shirley Raye decided to have Mark bring it up.

"How could you hire a ghost, Grampa?" Mark asks. "You don't believe in ghosts, do you? There are no such things as ghosts and goblins anyway."

Grampa sighed. "Mark, when I was a boy, there were no supersonic jets. I went to Africa on a ship. Man only dreamed of going to the moon, and we couldn't even imagine such things as heart transplants, microwave ovens, and high-tech computers. So you see, an old-fashioned ghost isn't such a hard thing for me to believe in after all."

> There must be a convincing explanation
> for anything that isn't realistic.

Many beginning writers mistakenly assume that because they are writing fiction, "anything goes." That's not true. Kids know that 10-year-old heroes and heroines won't drive cars, fight aliens with high-tech weapons, or have a cheetah for a pet. If fictional characters do those things, you'll have lots of explaining to do to make young readers "buy it." You'll have to convince an editor too.

> For those of you writing fantasy or science fiction,
> you must be <u>more</u> realistic than anyone else.

When writing stories about unicorns and centaurs living on distant planets in far away galaxies or long ago in "once upon a time," you'll have to obey the laws of that fictional universe. Before you can do so, you'll have to know what they are. Young readers want to become absorbed in the story. They don't want to turn the pages, wondering, "Why?" and "How come?" and "What's that?" Don't rely on coincidence or luck to resolve the story problem. That's not fair, and kids know it. Editors don't like the "It was all just a dream" ending, either.

REST STOP

Successfully Set the Stage

> The setting in a novel is almost as important as the characters and the plot.

If you think we're exaggerating, consider such places as Narnia, Redwall, and Hogwarts. For many young readers, these places are real—or should be. These are settings that keep young readers coming back for more. Every story, no matter how short, occurs in time and space. Show your readers where that is. Note that we suggest, "show." Don't tell. And when you show, do so briefly. Too much description slows down the narrative pace. Many kids just skip that part anyway. Don't be fond of your own words. Don't describe every tree, flower, sunset, and blade of grass. Kids like action and dialogue.

However, young readers do need to know where a story is taking place, particularly when they are reading a book with no illustrations. Setting matters. Can you imagine the drama of *Charlotte's Web* unfolding in some place other than Zuckerman's barn? Don't stick with visual descriptions only. Author E.B. White captures the rich aromas of the barnyard, the nice ones as well as the stinky ones. His sensory descriptions bring the barn to life for young readers. It's easy to write a creepy story that takes place in the woods or in an old haunted house. But what about a scary story that takes place in an ordinary town or school setting? That will take more effort on your part.

> If used properly, the setting will enhance
> character development and suggest plot ideas.

Grampa and the Ghost is set in Lincoln, Illinois, where Shirley Raye and her family used to live—on Pekin Street, just like the Gaffneys. The characters' names were taken randomly from the phone book. When Tallulah reminisces about her life in "old Postville" and tells the youngsters about a lawyer named Lincoln christening the town with the juice of a watermelon, she is only telling what any informed Lincoln resident can tell you. Even the imagery in the novel was inspired by having lived in central Illinois:

> *For Sibyl, the rest of the morning seemed to crawl along like one*
> *of the woolly worms that inch their way slowly across the Illinois*
> *roads and sidewalks in the fall.*

Week 5

Full Speed Ahead. You're Almost There

> You've taken a huge step toward a great accomplishment.
> You're doing it. Keep going!

Wrap up your writing this week. You may be done with your manuscript already. If so, what's next? Keep rewriting and polishing. Reconsider your book's opening. Is it the sort that will intrigue a busy editor? Are your scene transitions smooth? Do you keep the narrative flowing? Does your story conclusion satisfy?

Look at the Estimates sheet on page 20 that you filled out for word count, length of chapters, action scenes, dialogue, etc. Structure your manuscript to be similar to what's been successful on the market.

Assignment

If you are not finished, keep plugging away with your five pages per day.

REST STOP

How to Hook 'Em and Tantalize

We've had editors tell us more than once that the first paragraph or first 60 words of a manuscript is all they read before making a decision to reject it or keep reading. In our day and age, when children read books less than in the past, you don't have the luxury of starting with a leisurely, "Once upon a time," and giving lots of backstory before introducing your hero or heroine and the conflict.

> Bait your reader with some tasty morsel in the first 60 words.
> It will be worth the effort.

Keep in mind that editors get THOUSANDS of submissions each month. They can afford to be choosy. Somewhere in the slush pile on their desks (or stacked on the floor, the shelves, or the table in the middle of the room), they will find another manuscript that hooks them immediately. You want the editor to wonder, "What happens next?" and turn the page. So how do you do that?

> Start in the middle of an action scene. Say something intriguing or unusual in the very first sentence. Introduce a problem in the first paragraph.

In his book, *The 38 Most Common Fiction Writing Mistakes (And How to Avoid Them)*, author Jack M. Bickham writes, "Every good story starts at a moment of threat." Consider the opening line of the perennial children's favorite, *Charlotte's Web.*

> *"Where's Papa going with that ax?" said Fern to her mother as they were setting the table for breakfast.*
>
> *"Out to the hog house," replied Mrs. Arable. "Some pigs were born last night."*
>
> *"I don't see why he needs an ax," continued Fern who was only eight.*
>
> *"Well," said her mother, "one of the pigs is a runt. It's very small and weak, and it will never amount to anything. So your father has decided to do away with it."*
>
> *"Do away with it?" shrieked Fern. "You mean kill it? Just because it's smaller than the others?"*

In less than 100 words, author E.B. White successfully grabs his readers. You care about what's going to happen. You know too that Fern is going to be an admirable heroine. Youngsters will read on, hoping Fern will save that runty pig.

Here's the opening paragraph of Shirley Raye's middle grade novel, *Grampa and the Ghost.*

> *When Mark finished writing the ad for the newspaper, it read: Wanted: Professional ghost to help write autobiographical adventure story. Contact W. Gaffney, 123 Pekin Street, Lincoln, IL. Had he known what problems these simple words would cause, 10-year-old Mark might have dropped the whole idea of advertising for a ghostwriter in the first place. But he didn't know.*

In exactly 60 words, she introduces the main character and the story premise, hinting at the mishap to follow. Many youngsters will wonder, what's a ghostwriter? Why does Mark want to hire one? What's going to happen next?

Opening paragraphs are equally important when writing nonfiction for children. Maybe even more so. You don't want the book to read like a dry encyclopedia article. And you certainly don't want the editor to read the first line of the text ("George Washington was the first President of the United States."), then shrug and say, "So what?"

> You want an editor to raise her eyebrows and exclaim,
> "I didn't know that!"

Here's how Shirley Raye opened her nonfiction chapter book, *The Alamo*.

> *The Texas colonists were angry—very angry. In September of 1835 more than thirty thousand Americans were living in Texas. They called themselves "Texians." For a long time they had been urging Andrew Jackson, president of the United States, to buy the vast territory from Mexico. They desperately wanted to be free from the country's heavy taxes and unfair laws. Many of the men who immigrated to Texas were sons and grandsons of soldiers who had fought the British redcoats in the American Revolution.*

In less than 85 words, she gets the reader's attention, establishes the story premise, and sets the tone for the book.

> When writing nonfiction readers, which are often 1,000 words or less, you must set the stage and captivate the reader in only a few sentences.

In Jennifer's nonfiction reader, *Man O'War, Best Race Horse Ever*, she provides information and hints at something unusual.

> *Man o'War was a great race horse. Some say he was the greatest*
> *ever. He was born in 1917. But he didn't look like a racehorse then!*

What was wrong with him, some youngsters will wonder? Why was he considered the greatest racehorse of all? That's enough to keep them reading.

REST STOP ## Take the Reader Along with Easy Transitions

> The word *transition* means "the act of passing from one place to another."

You must move your characters from one scene to the next and from one chapter to the next. Do so smoothly. This is a skill that takes careful crafting. Using the "act of passing" image, don't let your characters run smack into a closed door and have to fumble with the doorknob to get into the next scene or chapter. You want them to pass effortlessly through one room to the next.

In her first draft of *Grampa and the Ghost*, Shirley Raye occasionally depicted Sibyl or Tallulah moving slowly and deliberately from one scene to the next. The narrative seemed to plod along in these spots. She decided to follow kids' TV programming as a guideline. Young viewers are whisked in and out of commercials and back to lively action scenes already in progress.

> If kids can keep up with the quick-paced scene changes on TV,
> then they can certainly handle it in a book.

However, your transition can't be so fast that the reader stops and asks, "What happened? Where are they now?" You need a transition to signal that time has passed.

> Be sure to use "bridge" words and phrases that carry
> your reader easily from one scene to the next.

Here are a few examples:

"Then the sky grew dark."

"Later Kate spiked the ball, again."

"Becky had that same strange look on her face when I visited her the next day."

> You need transitions in nonfiction too.
> These signal a change in subject matter, content, or time
> or indicate that you're leaving one main idea and moving on.

"Now scientists are trying to find a giant squid-alive."
"As summer turns to fall, the armadillo digs a home."
"This time, the Redcoats did shoot at Betty Zane."

An editor asked Jennifer to write a stronger transition for two paragraphs in her nonfiction manuscript *The Kraken* (which Thomson Gale released in 2008). Jennifer had written this paragraph about the giant squid in pop culture:

> *The Krakken in the TV series Ben 10 is a creature that lives in a lake and stays ready to defend it.*
> *Krakens, either alone or as a team of beasts, have been featured in many games, such as the role-playing game Dungeons & Dragons and computer games like Total Annihilation: Kingdoms and Age of Mythology.*

Jennifer crafted a better transition by picking up the reference to TV in the first paragraph and working it into the beginning sentence of the second paragraph.

> *The Krakken in the TV series Ben 10 is a massive creature that lives in a lake and stays ready to defend it and her giant egg.*
> *Books, movies, and television shows have established the fame of the Kraken in modern popular culture. As a result, collectible toy sets and a variety of games present the creature as a star character. Krakens, either alone or as a team of beasts, have been featured in many games, such as the role-playing game Dungeons & Dragons and computer games like Total Annihilation: Kingdoms and Age of Mythology.*

REST STOP

How to Craft Great Conclusions

The ideal ending will be so satisfying that the reader will wish the book hadn't ended, or a youngster might eagerly ask his parent, "Read it again?!"

Despite the roller coaster of emotions you may construct in your picture book or middle grade novel, it's important to end the story on an upbeat note. Children today have enough unsatisfying conclusions in real life. They shouldn't have to put up with them in books too. As we stated earlier, an ending doesn't have to be perfectly happy to be satisfying. But the ending should be hopeful, and justice should prevail. It should be logical based on the characters' lives, actions they've taken, and problems they've faced.

> A satisfying story conclusion will take into account each of the plot points.
>
> CHARACTER + ACTION + CONFLICT + CLIMAX + RESOLUTION

In Shirley Raye's picture book, *Blind Tom, The Horse that Helped Build the Great Railroad* (which Mountain Press Publishing published in 2009), the ending is pleasing because it shows the reader how the end of one thing can be the beginning of another.

A photographer took a picture of the railroad workers in front of the train tracks. Who do you suppose was also in the picture?

Blind Tom! He stood in the back with his friends, the iron men. This was the end of Blind Tom's hard work, but it was a new beginning for America.

Some picture books have a full circle plot in which the book ends at the same point in a cycle or with the same kind of event that started the story. A great example is *If You Give A Mouse A Cookie* by Laura Numeroff. Jennifer used the full circle structure in *Amazing Armadillos*. An adult armadillo goes out on a summer's night to hunt for food. She smells danger, but she knows just what to do. At the end, her four pups go out to hunt for food on a summer's night. Like their mother, they smell danger, but they know just what to do.

In Jennifer's book, *There Goes Turtle's Hat,* the wind sends a turtle's hat sailing through the zoo. Finally a gnu glues it on the turtle's head. The book ends with a picture of the turtle swirling through the air, because now when the wind blows turtle's hat, the turtle sails away with it. Kids seem to love the funny ending that's logical—in an offbeat way.

Week

6

More You Must Know About Marketing

This is one of the most important weeks of your successful writing plan. You've written the book. Now let it rest. Set it aside for a week. In the meantime, you're going to immerse yourself in market analysis.

Why should you bother with market analysis?
Because you're trying to break into print, and publishing is a business.

Even if an editor adores your submission, she must convince the marketing department that it will make money. The more "ammunition" you provide to help her accomplish this, the more likely you are to get a contract.

Benefit From Calendars

Calendars are one of the most valuable marketing tools
for children's book writers.

From editorial calendars to Hallmark calendars to specialized curriculum calendars, knowing how to use them can increase your chances of selling your manuscript. Used wisely, they can also increase your book sales. Savvy freelancers always mine calendars to increase their magazine article and story sales. Take a few lessons from them. Consider it as adding "seasoning" to your manuscript to make it more palatable to an editor.

Many stories and nonfiction topics can be tied to a particular date, such as the 4th of July or Thanksgiving. Women's History Month is in March, an opportune time for Shirley Raye to schedule speaking engagements and book signings for her *Patriots in Petticoats: Heroines of the American Revolution* (released by Random House in 2004).

Fortunately for the nonfiction writer, such anniversaries roll around every year. That means there's always a certain time of year when your title has great market potential. Shirley Raye's Lewis and Clark reader was released specifically to coincide with the 200th anniversary of the Corps of Discovery's historic expedition. The release date for *Blind Tom, The Horse that Helped Build the Great Railroad* coincided with President Lincoln's bicentennial and the 140th anniversary of the Golden Spike Ceremony in Promontory Point, Utah. Teachers and librarians are always looking for books with holiday themes, even for holidays like April Fool's Day, St. Patrick's Day, and Halloween.

> Fiction writers can benefit from anniversaries too.

Jennifer's *There Goes Turtle's Hat* takes place in a zoo. Chase's Calendar of Events, found in most libraries, provides lists of observances such as National Zoo Month.

The Goldmine of Current Events

Shirley Raye sold *Pigeon Hero!* to Simon & Schuster partly because she pointed out that there was very little World War II material for first graders. However, elementary students across the country had been helping to raise funds for the new memorial in Washington, D.C. Her book *The Alamo* came out to coincide with the Disney movie of the same name. Author Madge Harrah pitched her middle grade novel *Comet's Luck* to coincide with the return of Halley's Comet.

Discover the Wealth in School Curricula

Most textbook companies and publishers of educational materials and school library books have a calendar of school themes and topics that are covered by teachers in classrooms across the country. Did you know that Music in Our Schools month is observed nationwide each March and that September is dedicated to Character Building? Tie your topic to a curriculum theme, and it will sell more quickly and stay in print much longer. After all, a new crop of children start first grade annually. And, each year, there's a new herd of middle school youngsters and so on. Do you see the income potential for a good book with a school tie-in?

Assignment

Search online for your state's curriculum or content standards.
Look for important dates and themes that you can mention in your query or cover letter as curriculum or current event tie-ins.

Identify Your Best Chances

Assignment

Look in *Writer's Market* for the Book Publishers Subject Index.
Find the Children's / Juvenile section. Or look in the Category Index at the back
of *Book Markets for Children's Writers* to find a match for your story.
Several categories may apply to your manuscript.

You can scan the information for a publisher and quickly eliminate those that would not be a good match for your manuscript. If you see "Agented submissions only," and you don't have an agent to submit for you, move on to the next publisher. There are plenty who do not require you to have an agent.

You need to find publishers who accept simultaneous submissions, which means they will look at your manuscript even if you also send it to other publishers. Sometimes the listing will have "Accepts simultaneous submissions if identified," which means you are supposed to inform them that it is with other publishers. Most writers don't do this because editors admit it prejudices them a bit against the manuscript. The worst thing that could happen if you don't admit to simultaneously submitting a manuscript would be that two publishers want to buy your manuscript, and you then have to confess and reject one of them. That's actually a dilemma most writers would love to have. Yet, if it concerns you, then state in your cover letter, "This is a simultaneous submission."

The guidelines for a publisher will state what to submit, such as "complete manuscript" or "query with first chapter" or "query with synopsis." A synopsis is a condensed version of your story told in present tense. Many editors like a

20-word (or so) blurb for your story, similar to the blurb on the back of a book jacket, followed by a 50-word synopsis that includes the who, what, when, where, and why of your story.

Go to publishers' websites, which also have guidelines for writers. Check out their current catalogs. Read any available pages of the books to get a feel of the tone and style of the publisher.

The Secret of Tone and Style

In many cases, book publishers have a "tone and style" all their own. For beginners, this can be hard to discern. It's important to spend considerable time in the library or bookstores actually looking at books and reading them, as we suggested in Week 1. What do we mean exactly by tone and style? They are the flavor and feel of a manuscript.

Tone can be emotional or informative. Are you trying to explain something to youngsters? Are you trying to make them laugh or cry or persuade them—through fiction or nonfiction—not to take drugs, or to share their toys?

Another element of tone is distance. Are you writing in the first person in a conversational tone? Then you are "close" to your reader. On the other hand, if you're writing a 300-page nonfiction book on the Children's Crusade with lots of facts and maps, the distance between you and your reader might be considerable. Neither is wrong. However, some companies like chummy, friendly books. Others want books which are written with an authoritative, teaching tone.

Tone is closely related to style. Often people wearing tuxedos and expensive gowns act more formally than those wearing jeans and sweatshirts. It's the same with books. *Number the Stars* by Lois Lowry, *Snow Treasure* by Marie McSwigan, and *Pigeon Hero!* by Shirley Raye Redmond all have World War II themes, but they differ in tone and style. Not coincidentally, they are each published by different book companies, too.

<u>Assignment</u>

As you research publishers, match your manuscript to a house
that publishes books somewhat similar in style and tone to yours.

Conquer Those Query and Cover Letters

A query letter is a letter addressed to a specific editor or agent
that asks if he or she would be interested in seeing your manuscript.

It is well worth your time and effort to learn to write concise but intriguing query letters. Many publishers will not consider complete manuscripts. They want to see query letters. These are nothing more than letters of inquiry—asking an editor if she'd be interested in reading your manuscript.

> The purposes of a good query letter are to:
> - BAIT the editor,
> - INFORM the editor,
> - PITCH your manuscript to the editor, and
> - SELL you—as an author—to the editor.

At the back of this book, we've included examples of some letters to editors—Shirley Raye's query to Mountain Press Publishing and a cover letter that accompanied her giant squid manuscript. We use a similar four-paragraph letter each time. Note that in the cover letter, Shirley Raye didn't provide information about her publishing credits because the editor had already purchased a previous manuscript from her and had requested the giant squid manuscript after considering the query letter.

We recommend that you ALWAYS query, even if an editor accepts unsolicited manuscripts. Why? Because if the editor replies positively to your query letter, you can write "REQUESTED MANUSCRIPT" on the outside of the mailing envelope when you send it in. Your requested submission will not go in the dreaded "slush pile" (the stacks of unsolicited manuscripts sent "over the transom"). It will be placed on the editor's desk as soon as it arrives.

The query also saves money. Mailing a query letter so the editor can respond to you is cheaper than mailing the manuscript itself.

A cover letter is similar to a query letter.
It accompanies a complete manuscript and reads, for instance:
"Enclosed for your consideration is my 700-word picture book,
Goose Eats a Pickle, fiction for ages 4-8."

A query or a cover letter should be one page, single-spaced, with 1-inch margins. Double space between paragraphs and use a block format with no indentations. Use a common type and font, such as Times New Roman at 12 point. Include your name, address, email address, phone number, and website, if you have one. If a publisher's guidelines require an SASE (self-addressed stamped envelope), enclose one inside the envelope you mail to the editor.

Writer's Market has samples of good and bad query and cover letters, as well as guidelines for correctly formatted manuscripts.

Format Like a Pro

Correct manuscript format requires double-spaced text throughout and margins 1¼ inches all around. Copies of the first two pages of some of Jennifer's manuscripts are at the back of this book. Notice that the format of the first page is different from the format of the second page. A great book on formatting manuscripts for a wide range of writing projects is *Every Page Perfect* by Mary Lynn.

Week

7

Your Chance to Polish & Revise

Remember, don't skip this week of revision. Clean up that sloppy copy. A professional presentation is essential for attracting an editor's eye.

> Rigorous revision is often what separates the published writers
> from the unpublished ones. Do not resent revision.

Learn to enjoy polishing your prose. The sense of power you acquire when you learn to control and edit your writing is exhilarating. Since you wrote quickly and under pressure, you can be certain considerable revision will be required.

But don't pick your story to death. Be willing to accept the best you can do now. In his book *The 38 Most Common Fiction Writing Mistakes (And How to Avoid Them)*, author Jack M. Bickham advises:

> *One of the hardest things a writer has to do is to learn how to*
> *be self-critical (which leads to improvement) but not picky, worri-*
> *some or fretful. For all those negative, self-doubting attitudes are*
> *self-destructive.*

Assignment

Complete one task each day on the following checklist.

X Eliminate unnecessary characters. If you introduced a character in early scenes, and then dropped him or her, do you need that character at all? If so, pick him or her up again in later scenes. If not, eliminate the character completely. *Pawnbroker — AIF*

_____ Look at the Estimates sheet (page 20). Structure your manuscript to be somewhat in line with what's been successful on the market. Look at the lists on pages 7 and 8. Does your story appeal?

_____ Tie up any loose threads. Check your plot chart again. Did you hint at danger or mystery, but not develop that plotline or follow up?

_____ Be consistent. Does your protagonist still have blue eyes, or have they suddenly become brown? Have you been consistent with your spelling of Sacagawea (the preferred spelling used by the U.S. Mint), or did you switch to Sacajawea? Did you plan to have a character escape from a patio door, but no character has gone in or out that door before?

_____ Replace utility words. Those are the ones we use too often, and yet they tell us nothing. Such words include *wonderful, funny,* and *beautiful.* These are vague and do not convey specific meanings. Other utility words include *good, bad, great, fine, mad,* and *things.* Replace weaker verbs such as *talk* with stronger verbs such as *gabbed* or *argued.* Instead of *walk,* show us how he walked, using *strutted, ambled,* or *strolled.*

_____ Polish your grammar, punctuation, spelling, and sentence structure. Use the Spell Check and Grammar Check functions on your computer. Fix all sentence fragments and misplaced modifiers. Eliminate overuse of words such as *was* and *that.* Look for adverbs that end with "*ly.*" Replace the verb in the sentence with a stronger one that eliminates the need for the adverb. For example, change "he moved slowly" with "he limped," or "he inched his way." For help with grammar and punctuation, go to: http://www.grammarbook.com.

_____ Consider your paragraphs one by one. Are they tightly-focused? Are the transitions smooth? Does your sentence structure fit the age you're writing for, or is it too complex? Are your word choices age-appropriate and accurate? For example, when Shirley Raye polished her Lewis and Clark manuscript, she realized she had misused the words *marmot* and *woodchuck* to describe two different rodents. Actually, these two words refer to the same animal.

Congratulations. You Did It!
You wrote a children's book manuscript.
You took the biggest step toward
making your dream come true.

The
Authors

Shirley Raye Redmond

Shirley Raye Redmond is an award-winning writer and frequent conference speaker. She has sold more than 21 books and over 450 magazine and newspaper articles. Her children's book, *Lewis and Clark: A Prairie Dog for the President* (Random House) has sold more than 170,000 copies and was a Children's Book of the Month Club main selection in 2003. *Tentacles! Tales of the Giant Squid* (Random House, 2003) has also sold more than 160,000 copies. *Pigeon Hero!* (Simon and Schuster) won an Oppenheim Toy Portfolio Gold Book Award in 2004. *Patriots in Petticoats* (Random House) was named one of the best children's books of 2005 by Bank Street College of Education.

http://readshirleyraye.com

Jennifer McKerley

Jennifer McKerley enjoys writing fiction and nonfiction for all ages. Before she wrote children's books, she wrote magazine and newspaper articles. Random House published her nonfiction books *Man o' War, Best Racehorse Ever* and *Amazing Armadillos*, which Bank Street College of Education named one of the best children's books of 2010. *Goblins*, *The Kraken*, *Hydra*, and *Swamp Monster* were released by Thomson Gale, and Picture Window Books published her two fiction titles, *There Goes Turtle's Hat* and *Rules of the Net*.

www.jenniferguessmckerley.com

Samples

Query Letter

Cover Letter

Manuscript Format for a Reader

Format for a Longer Manuscript

Shirley Raye Redmond
Mailing address
Phone number
Email address

Date

Beth Parker
Mountain Press Publishing
PO Box 2399
Missoula, MT 59806

Dear Beth Parker:

Would you be willing to look at my 32-page picture book manuscript entitled, ***Where's Blind Tom Today?*** It is the true story about a horse that played a role in building the transcontinental railroad from Omaha, Nebraska, to Promontory Summit, Utah. This tale about an obscure, but all-American "horse hero" has child appeal and would be marketable to adult "trainiacs" at the nearly 300 railroad museums in the United States with bookstores/gift shops. It is <u>not</u> anthropomorphized, and the title's query was the telegraph operator's way of asking how many miles of track had been laid each day.

Two summers ago, I attended a lively reenactment of the Golden Spike Ceremony in Promontory. The 140th celebration will be observed in 2009, the same year as the bicentennial of President Lincoln's birth. The railroad was one of Lincoln's dream projects, but he never lived to see it completed. The Lincoln Bicentennial would provide many opportunities to promote the book through a variety of venues, such as the Golden Spike National Historic Site in Utah, which receives thousands of visitors each year.

Currently, there are no children's books about Blind Tom on the market. Past titles about the building of railroads are chapter books for older readers, such as ***The Transcontinental Railroad*** by Elaine Landau (Franklin Watts 2005) and ***Railroad Fever*** (National Geographic Books 2004). ***Full Steam Ahead*** by Blumberg and ***10-Day Mile*** by Fraser were both published in 1996 and are now out of print.

I have several nonfiction children's books in stores now. ***Patriots in Petticoats: Heroines of the American Revolution*** (Random House) was named one of the best children's books of 2005 by the Bank Street College of Education in New York. ***Lewis & Clark: A Prairie Dog for the President*** (Random Step Into Reading) has sold more than 130,000 copies and is recommended by the Lewis & Clark Trail Association. ***Pigeon Hero***! (Simon & Schuster) was an Oppenheim Best Book Gold Medal Winner for 2004. The title sells in venues such as the National D-Day Museum in New Orleans.

I'm a professional member of the Society of Children's Book Writers and Illustrators, Women Writing the West, the Albuquerque chapter of Sisters in Crime, Southwest Writers, the Los Alamos Historical Society and the New Mexico Book Association.

Sincerely,

Shirley Raye Redmond
Mailing address
Phone number
Email address

Date

Editor's Name, Title (if any)
Publishing House
Address
City, State and Zip

Dear Editor's Name:

What has jaws so strong that it can snap a wooden oar in two with just one bite, is as long as two school buses, and has the largest eyes of any creature on earth? The elusive giant squid!

Few people have ever seen this monster of the deep, and no one has ever captured a healthy, living specimen. Sailors told tall tales about the monster that chased ships, stretching its giant arms around the vessels and pulling them down into the sea. In fact, most people thought the giant squid was only a myth. But the giant squid is real, and researchers are actively pursuing the capture of a live one—using sperm whales and special cameras attached to the whales' backs.

Enclosed is my 900-word nonfiction manuscript about this elusive creature. I think it would be suitable as a level three reader for your Step into Reading line. Elementary students across the country study sea life each year as part of their science curriculum. This book would appeal to parents and teachers, as well as those youngsters interested in unique marine creatures. My information was obtained from Richard Ellis's book, *The Search for the Giant Squid*, and from Dr. Clyde Roper of the Smithsonian Institute, who received a National Geographic grant to search for the creature near Australia.

I look forward to hearing from you.

Sincerely,

Jennifer McKerley
123 Street
City, State Zip
Phone
Email

Step Into Reading, Step 3
Random House
950 words, 48 pages

AMAZING ARMADILLOS

by

Jennifer McKerley

(pp. 4-5)

The armadillo comes out

to hunt on a summer night.

(Say ar-muh-**DIH**-loh)

Her walk is slow and clumsy.

She stands up on her back legs

to listen and sniff the air.

Uh-oh!

She smells danger.

(6-7)

A bobcat is on the prowl.

Still the armadillo

knows what to do.

Like a digging machine,

she rips the ground

with her claws.

Quickly she disappears

inside the hole.

The bobcat finally gives up.

That's good for the armadillo.

All that digging

has made her hungry.

(8-9)

The armadillo grunts and

squeals and hunts with

her nose in the dirt.

Armadillos do not see well.

So she uses her sharp senses of

smell and hearing to find food.

Tonight, she picks up the

the scent of a beetle.

Yum!

Jennifer McKerley
123 Street
City, State Zip
Phone
Email

Picture Book Biography
48 pages
1,000 words
Author's Note: 251 words

SECRETS AND SLIPPERS

by

Jennifer McKerley

It was 1962 at the Academy Awards. Actress Audrey Hepburn held her breath.
The host opened the envelope to read the winner for Best Actress in a movie. "Miss
Audrey Hepburn for Roman Holiday," he announced.

Applause filled the theater as the actress walked up to receive her award. "I'm
truly, truly grateful," she said, "and terribly happy."

The famous star felt blessed. It seemed like just yesterday that she was a girl in
the middle of a war. Though glamour and excitement now filled her life, she never forgot
what she had seen and heard.

Audrey had her eleventh birthday on May 4, 1940. Yet her best present came five days later when she watched her favorite ballerina, Margo Fonteyn, dance.

Audrey loved dancing. It soothed her. When her father left the family six years earlier, her heart had broken. Then she took dancing lessons at her boarding school in England and discovered something. When she danced, she forgot sad things for a while. Now she was back home in Arnhem, Holland, and she longed to take lessons again.

Audrey couldn't take her eyes off Fonteyn as she soared across the stage. After the performance, Audrey presented tulips and roses to the star and told her she wanted to be a ballerina too. "It's what I dream about every night," she said. Audrey's heart filled with purpose. Around her though, the adults talked in worried whispers. They said war was coming to Arnhem.

The Second World War had started the year before. Adolf Hitler was the Chancellor of Germany. His Nazi soldiers had already conquered four countries, and Hitler wanted to rule all of Europe. Three hours after Fonteyn's performance ended, the Germans attacked Holland. The next morning, Audrey and her big brothers, Alex and Ian, peeked out the shutters of their home. Like a sea of gray, trucks and troops swept through the streets and took over Arnhem.

Inside, Audrey danced and pushed away her fright. Outside, everything changed. Nazi flags unfurled over schools. Dutch books were thrown away. Students had to learn German, and they could only read books that praised Hitler. Bicycles had once filled Arnhem's streets. Now tanks rumbled by, spewing exhaust onto the flower boxes. Nazi soldiers shouted orders at citizens and even moved in to live with Dutch families.

When German officers started living in Audrey's house, her family schemed and